I can't
get it
Mom.

you need to
keep t

Don't give

It's so hard.

I know
sweetie,

I know...

Let's do it
together.

To Sophia Marie.
You inspire me.

Ages 5 and up

Maren Green Publishing, Inc.
5525 Memorial Avenue North, Suite 6
Oak Park Heights, MN 55082

Library of Congress Control Number: 2007926559

Edited by Pamela Espeland
Text set in Journal Text
Illustrations created using pastels on Reeves paper

First Edition June 2007
10 9 8 7 6 5 4 3 2 1
Manufactured in China

ISBN 978-1-934277-12-6

www.marengreen.com

Child of Mine

52022

Written and illustrated by

Carrie Hartman

Maren Green Publishing, Inc.
Oak Park Heights, Minnesota

Child of mine . . .

little girl of mine...

At times you are so content.

You sing and smile.

But then...

...so quickly

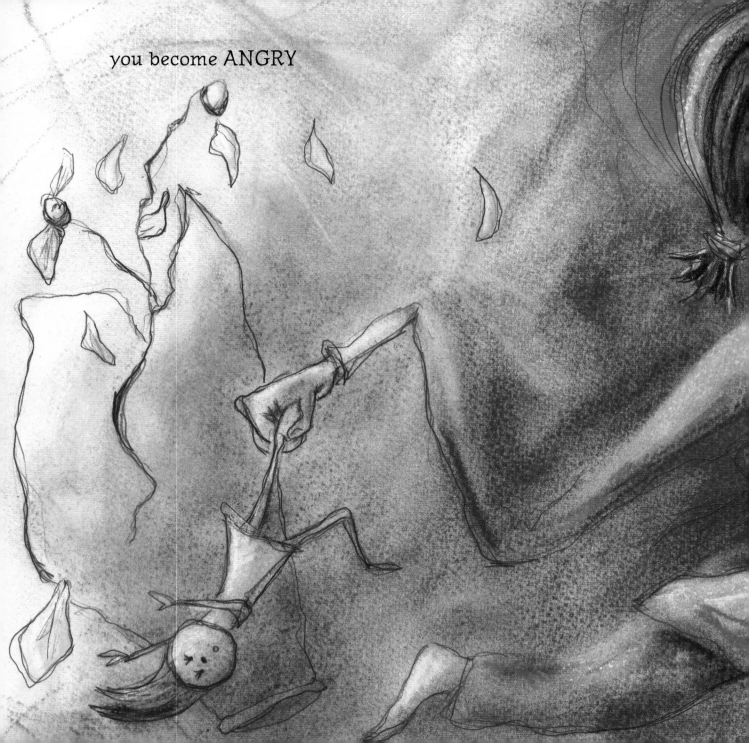

and I don't know why.

You yell

and throw things.

I know you are often sad and feel

alone.

This makes me sad, too.

I would do anything
to help you feel less
angry, sad, and alone.

Anything.

I cry for you.

I pray for you.

I wish that being a kid wasn't so hard for you.

I feel guilty sometimes for wishing
things were different or easier.

Easier not only for you,

but also for me.

Then I realize how much
you have given me.

Your giggles, your hugs,
your curiosity...

bring me happiness.

Because of you, I am a different person,

a better person.

I believe in you.

I know you will find a way to be happy,
and your life will be *beautiful*.

Child of mine . . .

AUTHOR'S NOTE

Child of Mine was inspired by my daughter, who proved to be a challenging child at an early age. My intent was to acknowledge and convey the emotions that accompany behavioral and emotional health issues. Daily life can be a rollercoaster of extreme highs and lows—frustration, anger, sadness, joy—not only for the child but also for the parent or caregiver. The message of this book is one of hope. If you're the parent of a spirited child, it's important to stay positive and focused on the good things, even on days when that's very h a r d to do. Believe in this unique and wonderful young person with whom you have been blessed. Believe in your child's ability to find his or her way through life and to be happy and successful. Have faith in your child's future. Celebrate your child's energy and creativity. Find comfort and hope where you can, perhaps on the pages of this book. Finally: Thank you, Sophia, for teaching me to be a better parent and daring me to be a better person.

$18 - 5 = 12$

let's try.
again

no I can't

$18 - 5 = 11$

you almost
have it.